back to
CHARM SCHOOL
more fun quilts from country threads

Mary Etherington and Connie Tesene

Martingale
Create with Confidence

Credits

President & CEO: Tom Wierzbicki

Editor in Chief: Mary V. Green

Managing Editor: Karen Costello Soltys

Technical Editor: Robin Strobel

Copy Editor: Marcy Heffernan

Design Director: Stan Green

Production Manager: Regina Girard

Illustrator: Laurel Strand

Cover & Text Designer: Shelly Garrison

Photographer: Brent Kane

Special thanks to Rosemary and Clifford Bailey of Snohomish, Washington, for generously allowing us to photograph in their home.

Mission Statement

Dedicated to providing quality products and service to inspire creativity.

Back to Charm School: More Fun Quilts from Country Threads
© 2011 by Mary Etherington and Connie Tesene

Martingale®
19021 120th Ave. NE, Suite 102
Bothell, WA 98011-9511 USA
ShopMartingale.com

Printed in China
16 15 14 13 12   8 7 6 5 4 3 2

Library of Congress Cataloging-in-Publication Data is available upon request.

ISBN: 978-1-60468-074-4

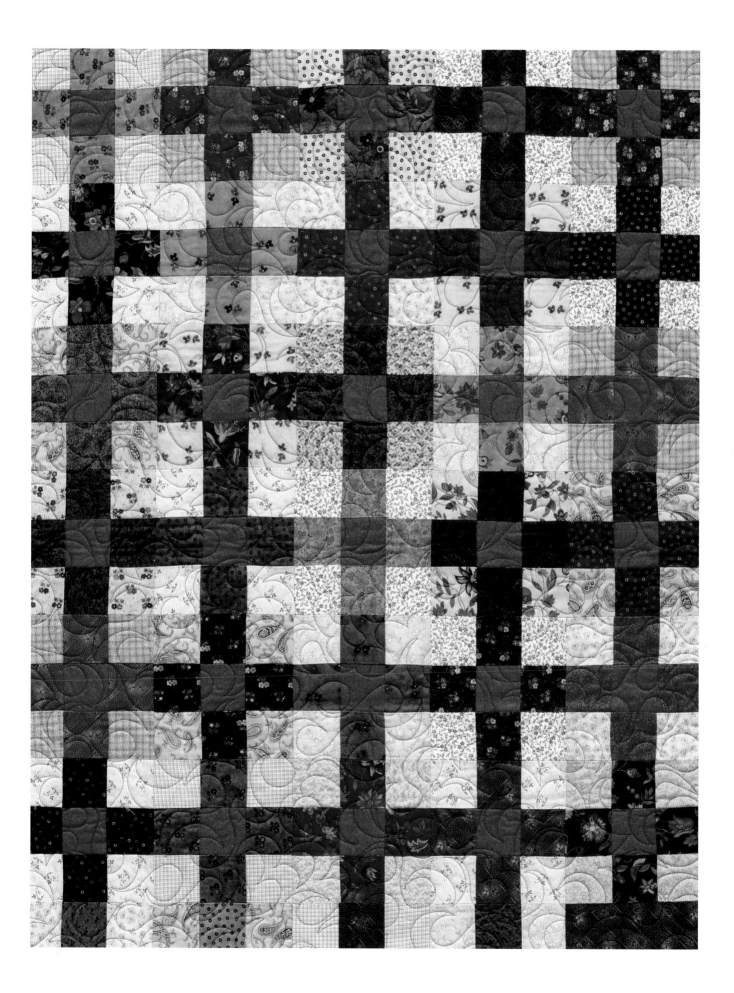

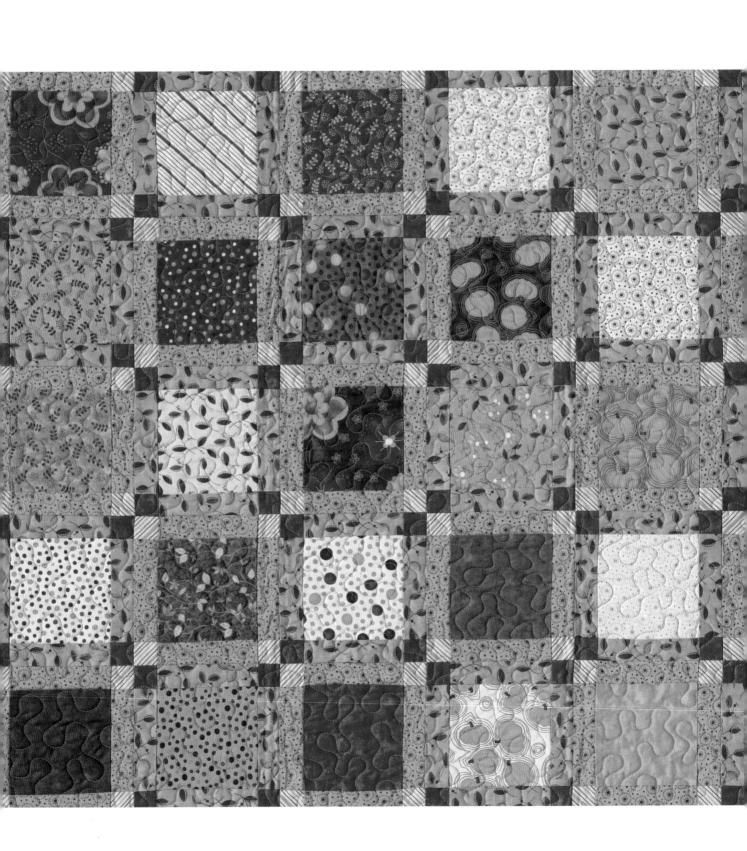

Contents

As with all forms of education, Charm School continues at Country Threads. When it began several years ago, we started using precut 5" charm squares in "baby steps" patterns such as simply sewing the squares together for a small project. Because our customers enjoyed it so much, we then challenged ourselves to use charm squares to make a different pattern every month. For several years we designed new projects for our customers until our friends at Martingale & Company compiled 19 charm projects in our book, *Country Threads Goes to Charm School* (2010). With the success of that book, we were

encouraged to keep experimenting with charm squares. And the projects became more fun with each one we made.

So here we are, another book later with more charm projects for you to enjoy. Some are more difficult than others, but we all need a challenge now and then. What better way to try something new than in a small quilt? Another reason we like making charm projects is that neither of us is an accomplished machine quilter, yet this small size is easy to handle in our sewing machines. Even we can machine quilt a charm quilt!

Country Threads has been in business in north-central Iowa for almost 29 years at the time we write this, and retirement looms in front of us. But we love coming to the quilt shop every day and can't imagine life without our staff and customers. The dogs and cats still greet our guests in the driveway, as they did when our first book, *Country Threads: The Quilt Shop Series*, was published by Martingale & Company in 1991. Our loyal friends and customers are still shopping, coming to camp, making quilts and rugs, and reading the *Goat Gazette*, our quarterly newsletter. Our online store makes it possible to shop 24/7, which has modernized our business. The farm continues to thrive with chickens, goats, geese, dogs, and cats living here with the quilt shop. We also love to garden and collect junk to display in the garden—our interests are many and varied, just like our customers' hobbies. We just don't have time to retire!

Welcome back to Country Threads, and thank you to our friends at Martingale & Company for again putting their trust in us to design projects that are fun for quilters to sew.

~ Mary and Connie

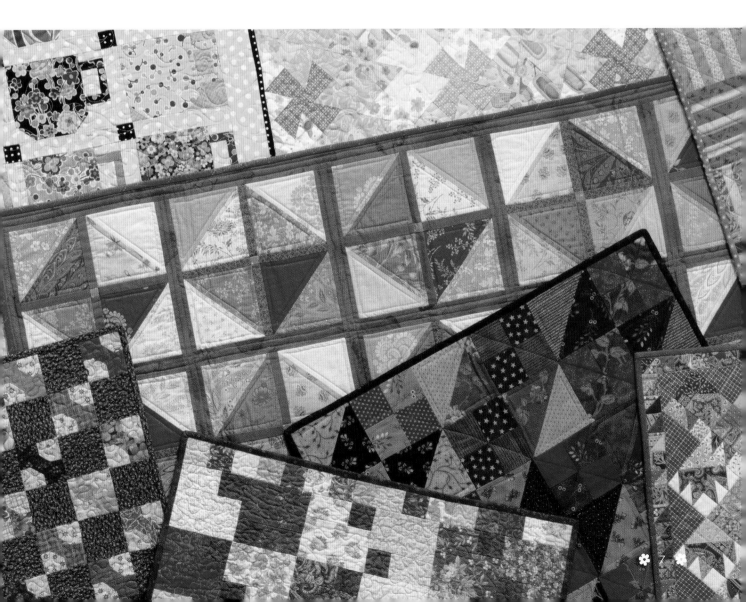

Quilt size: 24" x 24" ❀ Finished block: 8" x 8"

In these days of Evite and Facebook, it's becoming rare to receive a written invitation. But even if it involves no more than clicking on "accept," it's only polite and proper to respond to invitations in a timely manner. Of course, everyone will want to accept an invitation to see this charming little quilt!

MATERIALS

All yardages are based on 42"-wide fabric. Charm squares are 5" x 5".

36 charm squares in an assortment of light, medium, and dark values

¼ yard of black print fabric for binding

⅞ yard of fabric for backing

30" x 30" piece of batting

CUTTING

All measurements include ¼"-wide seam allowances.

From the black print fabric, cut:
3 strips, 2¼" x 42"

making do

If you don't have a set of precut charm squares, you'll need one fat eighth (9" x 20") each of four medium to dark red, four light gold, two medium to dark brown, two blue, and two green fabrics. Cut a total of 36 charm squares, 5" x 5", making about half lighter in value than the other half.

CREATING THE QUILT

Each block is made up of two matching half-square-triangle units and two matching four-patch units.

1. Pair nine light charm squares with nine dark charm squares. Trim each square to 4⅞" x 4⅞", and draw a diagonal line from corner to corner on the wrong side of the light fabrics.

2. Place a light square and a dark square from step 1 right sides together and stitch ¼" on each side of the line. Cut in half along the line, creating two matching triangle units. Press the seam allowances toward the darker fabric. Make nine pairs of half-square-triangle units (18 total).

Make 9
matching pairs.

3. Layer two charm squares, right sides together. Sew ¼" in from each side and cut in half, 2½" from the edge. Press the seam allowances toward the darker fabric.

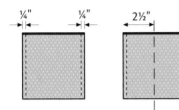

¼" ¼" 2½"

4. Layer the two units from step 3 right sides together with the light fabrics opposite the dark fabrics, matching the seams. Sew ¼" in from each side and cut in half, 2½" from the edge. Press the seam allowances open. You'll have two matching four-patch units.

2½"

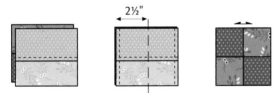

5. Repeat steps 3 and 4 to make nine pairs of four-patch units (18 total).

6. Pair two matching half-square-triangle units with two matching four-patch units to create one block. Sew the triangle units to the four-patch units as shown and press the seam allowances open. Sew the resulting matching units together and press the seam allowances open. Make a total of nine blocks.

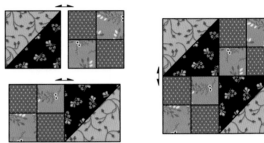

Make 9.

7. Arrange the blocks in three rows of three blocks each. Sew the blocks into rows, pressing the seam allowances open. Sew the rows together and press.

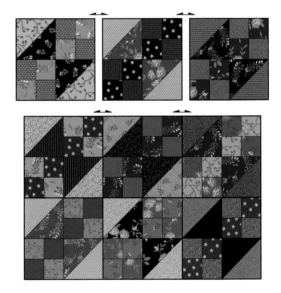

country sense

Because there are no borders on this quilt, it's all too easy for the seams to pull apart as you baste and quilt the top. To prevent this, stay stitch around the outside edge using a scant ¼" seam allowance.

8. Make a quilt back approximately 30" x 30". Layer the quilt top with batting and backing. Baste, and then quilt as desired. Trim the excess batting and backing and bind the quilt with the black print 2¼"-wide strips.

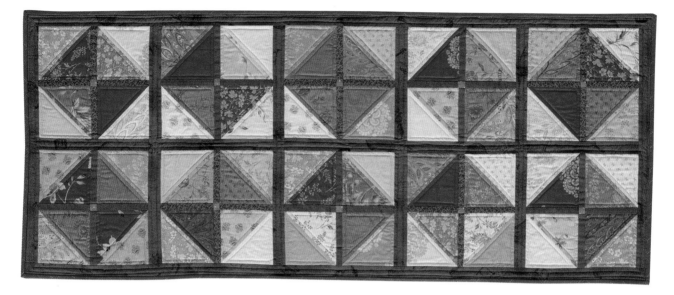

Quilt size: 20" x 48½" ✿ Finished block: 8½" x 8½"

MATERIALS

All yardages are based on 42"–wide fabric. Charm squares are 5" x 5".

40 assorted charm squares fairly evenly divided between light and dark values for blocks

⅔ yard of brown tone-on-tone fabric for wide sashing and outer border

⅛ yard *each* of two brown prints for narrow sashing in blocks

1 fat eighth (18" x 21") of grayish-blue fabric for cornerstones

⅓ yard of red fabric for binding

1¾ yards of fabric for backing

26" x 55" piece of batting

CUTTING

From *each* of the two brown prints, cut:
20 rectangles, 1" x 4½" (40 total)

From the grayish-blue fabric, cut:
10 squares, 1" x 1"

From the brown tone-on-tone fabric, cut:
8 strips, 1½" x 42"; crosscut into:
    5 rectangles, 1½" x 9"
    6 strips, 1½" x 18½"
    3 strips, 1½" x 42"

From the red fabric, cut:
4 strips, 2¼" x 42"

This rule makes us laugh because we usually use our fingers to eat cheese! How tacky is that? There is nothing tacky about this little quilt, however. It's just a small taste of country charm.

✿ 11 ✿

making do

If you don't have a set of precut charm squares, you'll need one fat quarter *each* of four assorted red, four assorted tan or off-white, and three medium- to dark-taupe fabrics.

CREATING THE QUILT

1. Pair 20 light charm squares with 20 dark charm squares, right sides together, and draw a diagonal line from corner to corner on the wrong side of the light squares.

2. Stitch ¼" on each side of the line. Cut in half along the line, creating two matching half-square-triangle units. Press the seam allowances toward the darker fabric. Trim the units to measure 4½" x 4½". Repeat to make 40 half-square-triangle units.

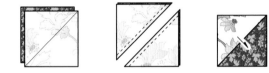

3. Arrange four half-square-triangle units, four brown 1" x 4½" rectangles, and one grayish-blue 1" square, being careful to orient the darker triangles toward the blue square. Sew the units together to make a block. Press the seam allowances toward the brown rectangles. Repeat to make 10 blocks.

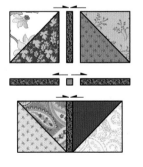

Make 10.

country back roads

A charm-school quilt doesn't have to have perfect blocks. In our sample there are a couple of blocks with the lighter fabric of a half-square-triangle unit facing the blue square. Would you notice if we hadn't mentioned it? We think an occasional deviation from the pattern adds a bit of interest, much like taking a side trip on a back road instead of staying on the interstate.

4. Sew together two blocks with a brown 1½" x 9" sashing rectangle in between. Repeat to make five rows of two blocks each. Sew the rows together, adding a brown 1½" x 18½" sashing strip between each row and at the top and bottom of the quilt top. Press the seam allowances toward the sashing.

5. Sew the three brown 1½" x 42" strips together end to end to make a long strip. Press the seam allowances open. From this long strip, cut two side borders, 1½" x 49". Sew the borders to the sides of the quilt top. Press the seam allowances toward the borders.

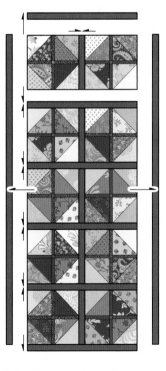

6. Make a quilt back approximately 26" x 55". Layer the quilt top with batting and backing. Baste, and then quilt as desired. Trim the excess batting and backing and bind the quilt with the red 2¼"-wide strips.

Break Off One
Bite-Sized Piece of Roll at a Time

Quilt size: 30" x 42" ❀ Finished block: 6" x 6"

Nine Patch blocks with light fabrics in the corners join to make a woven design. But it looks as though someone's taken a big bite out of the corner of the quilt!

MATERIALS

All yardages are based on 42"-wide fabric. Charm squares are 5" x 5".

34 assorted light-brown or white charm squares for blocks

34 assorted dark-value charm squares for blocks

9 assorted dark-red charm squares for blocks

½ yard of dark-blue print for unpieced block and binding

1½ yards of fabric for backing

36" x 48" piece of batting

CUTTING

All measurements include ¼"-wide seam allowances.

From *each* charm square, cut:
4 squares, 2½" x 2½" (136 dark, 136 light, and 36 red)*

From the dark-blue print, cut:
1 square, 6½" x 6½"

4 strips, 2¼" x 42"

*Keep squares of the same fabric together.

making do

If you don't have charm squares, you'll need one strip, 2½" x 42", *each* of nine assorted light-value fabrics and one strip, 2½" x 42", *each* of nine assorted dark-value fabrics. You'll also need ⅓ yard of one red print or one strip, 2½" x 41", *each* of three assorted red prints.

CREATING THE QUILT

Each block is made from four matching light-value squares, four matching dark-value squares, and one red square.

1. Arrange four matching light-value squares, four matching dark-value squares, and one red square into a Nine Patch block with the red in the center and the light-value squares in the corners. Sew the squares together and press as shown. Make 34 blocks. You'll have two red squares left over.

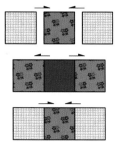 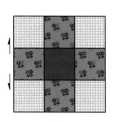

Make 34.

country style

We like the quirkiness of the unpieced block in this quilt, but if you want your quilt to look more symmetrical, make 35 Nine Patch blocks instead of 34 blocks. It takes one additional light-value charm square and one additional dark-value charm square. You'll only need ⅜ yard of dark-blue print since you won't need to cut the unpieced square.

2. Arrange the blocks in seven rows of five blocks in each row. In one corner of the quilt, place the dark-blue 6½" square. Sew the blocks into rows and press the seam allowances in opposite directions. Sew the rows together and press.

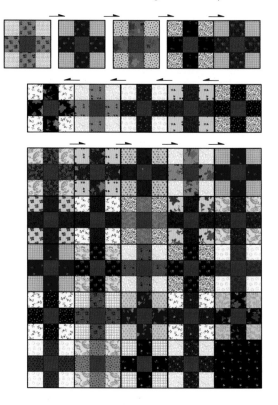

3. Make a quilt back approximately 36" x 48". Layer the quilt top with batting and backing. Baste, and then quilt as desired. Trim the excess batting and backing and bind the quilt with the dark-blue 2¼"-wide strips.

Better to Be Overdressed than Underdressed

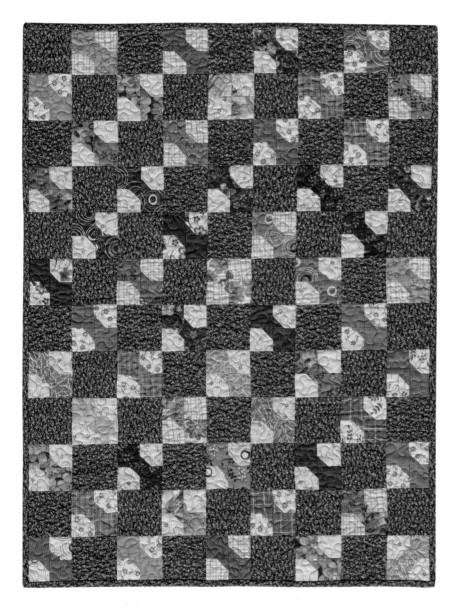

Spiffy little Bow Tie blocks dress up this quilt, but its country flair gives it a down-home feel.

Quilt size: 22½" x 30" ❀ Finished block: 2½" x 2½"

MATERIALS

All yardages are based on 42"-wide fabric. Charm squares are 5" x 5".

27 assorted dark-value charm squares for Bow Tie blocks

27 assorted light-value charm squares for Bow Tie blocks

⅞ yard of dark-purple print for unpieced blocks and binding

⅞ yard of fabric for backing

28" x 36" piece of batting

CUTTING

All measurements include ¼"-wide seam allowances.

From *each* of the assorted dark-value charm squares, cut:
4 squares, 1¾" x 1¾" (108 total)*
4 squares, 1⅛" x 1⅛" (108 total)*

From *each* of the assorted light-value charm squares, cut:
4 squares, 1¾" x 1¾" (108 total)*

From the dark-purple print, cut:
5 strips 3" x 42"; crosscut into 54 squares, 3" x 3"
4 strips, 2¼" x 42"

Keep squares of the same fabric together.

---

making do

If you don't have a set of precut charm squares, you'll need one fat eighth (9" x 21") *each* of 11 assorted dark-value prints; cut 10 squares, 1¾" x 1¾", and 10 squares, 1⅛" x 1⅛", from each. You'll also require one fat eighth each of nine assorted light-value prints; cut 12 squares, 1¾" x 1¾", from each. You'll have a couple of squares and some leftover fabric you can use for piecing the back of the quilt.

CREATING THE QUILT

Each Bow Tie block is made from four matching dark-value and two matching light-value squares.

1. Place a dark 1⅛" square on the corner of a light 1¾" square, right sides together. Stitch diagonally from corner to corner on the dark square; trim the outside corner of the connector square and press toward the corner. Refer to "Connector Squares" on page 74, if needed. Repeat with a second set of matching dark- and light-value squares.

Make 2.

2. Arrange the two units from step 1 with two matching dark-value 1¾" charm squares and sew the units together to make a Bow Tie block.

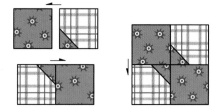

3. Repeat steps 1 and 2 to make 54 Bow Tie blocks.

4. Alternate the Bow Tie blocks and dark-purple 3" squares in 12 rows of nine blocks and squares in each row. We chose to orient (almost) all our Bow Tie blocks in the same direction, but there are many different ways to arrange them. Experiment! Sew the blocks into rows, pressing seam allowances toward the purple squares. Sew the rows together and press.

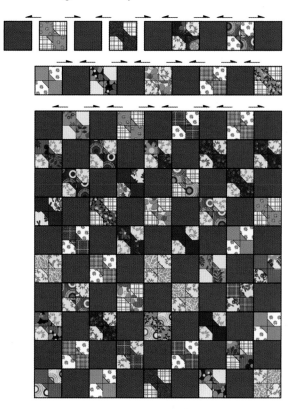

5. Make a quilt back approximately 26" x 36". Layer the quilt top with batting and backing. Baste, and then quilt as desired. Trim the excess batting and backing and bind the quilt with the dark-purple 2¼"-wide strips.

Never Leave the Table before the Other Guests

Quilt size: 15" x 24" ❀ Finished block: 3"x 3"

Etiquette notwith-
standing, no one
will want to leave a
table with this little
centerpiece on it.
They'll be too busy
admiring all the little
squares. No one will
guess strip-piecing
techniques make this
a quick and easy
project.

MATERIALS

All yardages are based on 42"-wide fabric. Charm squares are 5" x 5".

20 assorted medium- to dark-blue charm squares for blocks

20 assorted light-brown and gold charm squares for blocks

⅛ yard of dark-blue print for binding

⅝ yard of fabric for backing

21" x 30" piece of batting

CUTTING

All measurements include ¼"-wide seam allowances.

From each charm square, cut:
4 rectangles, 1¼" x 5" (80 dark and 80 light total)*

From the dark-blue print, cut:
3 strips, 2¼" x 42"

*Keep rectangles of the same fabric together.

making do

If you don't have a set of precut charm squares, you'll need
a *minimum* of 10 medium- to dark-blue strips, 2½" x 21", and
10 light-brown or gold strips, 2½" x 21". Cut each strip in half
lengthwise, and in step 1 on page 22, use the resulting 1¼" x 21"
strips to make 10 strip units.

CREATING THE QUILT

Each 16 Patch block is made from one dark- or medium-blue fabric and one light-brown or gold fabric.

1. Alternate and sew together two matching blue 1¼" x 5" rectangles and two matching brown or gold 1¼" x 5" rectangles to make a strip unit as shown. Press the seam allowances in one direction. Crosscut the unit into four segments, 1¼" x 5".

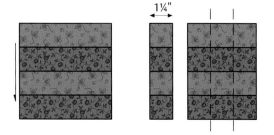

2. Rotate every other segment 180° and sew the segments together to make a 16 Patch block. Press the seam allowances in one direction.

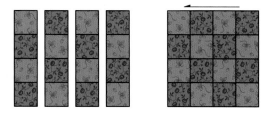

3. Repeat steps 1 and 2 with the remaining charm-square rectangles to make 40 blocks.

4. Arrange the blocks into eight rows of five blocks in each row, placing the blocks so the checkerboard pattern continues throughout the quilt. Sew the blocks into rows and press the rows in opposite directions. Sew the rows together and press.

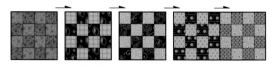

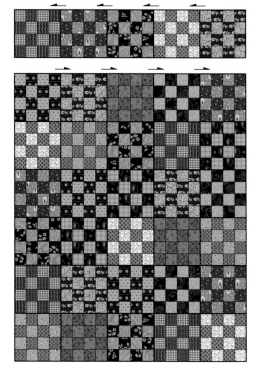

5. Make a quilt back approximately 21" x 30". Layer the quilt top with batting and backing. Baste, and then quilt as desired. Trim the excess batting and backing and bind the quilt with the dark blue 2¼"-wide strips.

Quilt size: 12" x 30" ❀ Finished block: 6" x 6"

MATERIALS

All yardages are based on 42"-wide fabric. Charm squares are 5" x 5".

40 *total* assorted charm squares divided roughly as follows: 12 bright red, 10 light value, 10 colonial blue, and 8 medium-brown prints

¼ yard of red fabric for binding

⅝ yard of fabric for backing

18" x 36" piece of batting

CUTTING

All measurements include ¼"-wide seam allowances.

From *each* charm square, cut:
2 squares, 2⅜" x 2⅜" (80 total)*
2 squares, 2" x 2" (80 total)*

From the red fabric, cut:
3 strips, 2¼" x 42"

Keep squares of the same fabric together.

It's easy. Just say, "Hi. I'm the person who can't stop making all those wonderful charm quilts." Well, maybe your car-repair place won't know who you are, but we bet most of your friends will!

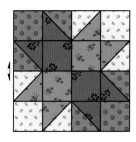

making do

If you don't have a set of precut charm squares, you'll need one fat eighth (9" x 21") *each* of six assorted bright-red prints, five assorted light-value prints, five assorted colonial-blue prints, and four assorted brown prints. Cut four squares, 2" x 2", and four squares, 2⅜" x 2⅜", from each fabric.

CREATING THE QUILT

Each block is made from two pairs of fabrics.

1. Pair up 2⅜" squares into darks and lights or accents and backgrounds, keeping the same fabrics together. In general, we paired a bright-red square with a medium-brown square and a colonial-blue square with a light-value square. You need to pair each fabric with one that contrasts with it.

2. Place a pair of charm squares from step 1 right sides together. Draw a diagonal line from corner to corner on the wrong side of the lighter square. Stitch ¼" on each side of the line. Cut apart on the line and press the seam allowances toward the darker triangles. Repeat with the remaining pairs of 2⅜" squares to make 20 sets with four matching half-square-triangle units in each set.

Make 20 sets
of 4 matching
triangle units
(80 total).

3. Arrange two matching half-square-triangle units with two matching 2" squares, being careful to orient them as shown. Sew the triangles and squares together, pressing the seam allowances toward the squares. Sew these units together and press seam allowances open. Repeat to make two identical units for each block (20 pairs total).

Make 20
matching pairs.

4. Pair two matching red/brown units from step 3 with two matching colonial-blue/light units. Arrange and sew together as shown. We like to press the seam allowances open since it helps the blocks lie flat when sewn together. Repeat to make 10 blocks.

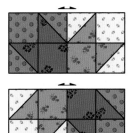

Make 10.

country charm

Not all of our blocks have red-and-blue stars. Two stars are all red and one is all blue. We like the random look this gives our quilt, so don't worry if your charm pack doesn't have the specified number of red and blue squares.

5. Sew the blocks together into five rows of two blocks each. Press the seam allowances open.

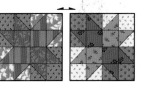

6. Make a quilt back approximately 18" x 36". Layer the quilt top with batting and backing. Baste, and then quilt as desired. Trim the excess batting and backing and bind the quilt with the red 2¼"-wide strips.

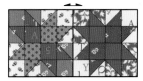

Our Honeycomb quilt reminds us of lots of elbows defiantly lined up on a table. Why do rules always make us want to do the opposite? Indulge your desire to do something different by making this unusual pattern. It looks terrific with your favorite charm pack, regardless of the colors or themes. If you haven't used templates or tried hand stitching, this is a perfect place to begin.

Quilt size: 20" x 28" ❀ Finished block: 4⅛" x 2"

MATERIALS

All yardages are based on 42"-wide fabric. Charm squares are 5" x 5".

31 charm squares in a variety of prints and colors

¼ yard of blue print for border

¼ yard of red-checked fabric for binding

1 yard of fabric for backing

26" x 34" piece of batting

Hand-sewing needle

Template plastic **OR** acrylic template for Church Windows (honeycomb shape, available at your local quilt shop or Country Threads)

CUTTING

All measurements include ¼"-wide seam allowances.

From each charm square, cut:
2 honeycomb shapes using pattern on page 29 (62 total)*

From the blue print, cut:
3 strips, 2½" x 42"

From the red-checked fabric, cut:
3 strips, 2¼" x 42"

*Refer to "Working with Templates" on page 74 if needed.

making do

Use all those leftover scraps of fabric you can't bear to throw away. You need 62 pieces measuring at least 2½" x 5". The more fabrics you use, the better the quilt! If you can't find a charm pack, don't keep fabric scraps, and therefore need to purchase yardage, we suggest a minimum of 12 different prints, so buy the smallest amount possible. Cut five or six honeycomb shapes from each fabric (62 total).

CREATING THE QUILT

1. On the wrong side of each honeycomb piece, use a pencil and a small ruler to lightly mark the short seam lines and the dots.

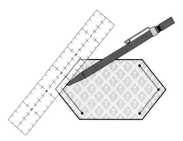

2. Using your sewing machine, sew the long sides of the honeycomb shapes together to make three rows with 12 honeycombs and two rows with 13 honeycombs. Do not stitch into the seam allowances, but backstitch at the beginning and end of each seam.

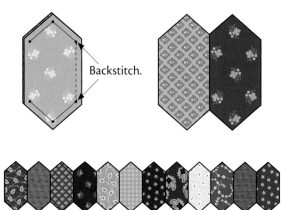

Backstitch.

Make 3.

Make 2.

3. Lay a 12-honeycomb row right sides together with a 13-honeycomb row and sew the rows together by hand, working on one small section at a time. Start and stop ¼" from the edge. Do not stitch into the seam allowance. Sew all the rows together in

this manner, alternating the longer rows with the shorter rows. Press the seam allowances open.

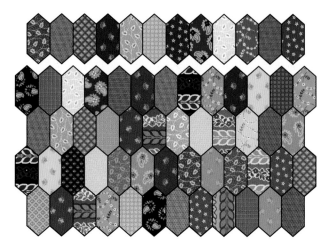

country know-how

Don't be intimidated by hand sewing! Yes, it takes more time than using a machine, but it's not at all difficult. Align the two pieces of fabric. Insert the needle at the dots and make a little backstitch. Then rock the needle up and down, in and out of the two layers of fabric, following the marked seam line. Stop when you reach the point and machine-stitched seam; pull the thread through so it lies flat on the fabric. If you pull the thread too taut, gently tug on the fabric a little so the thread loosens up.

Realign the edges of the fabrics and stitch along the seam line to the next point and machine-stitched seam. At the end of the row, take another little backstitch and cut the thread, leaving a small tail. The starting and stopping points will be secured when you stitch the borders to the quilt top. You'll be surprised how quickly you finish sewing the rows together.

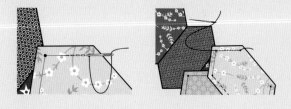

4. Trim the edges of the quilt to form a rectangle.

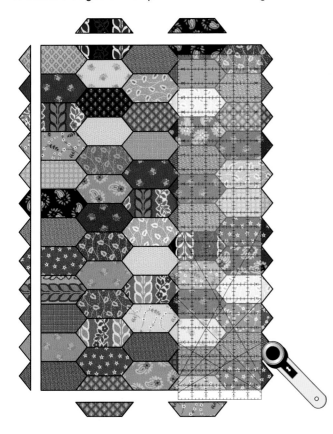

measurement. Sew them to the sides of the quilt and press the seam allowances toward the blue borders.

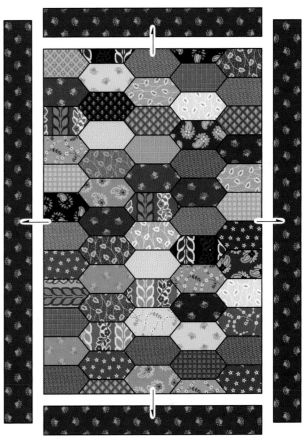

5. Measure the width of the quilt and cut two pieces from one of the blue 2½"-wide strips to this measurement. Sew them to the top and bottom of the quilt, pressing the seam allowances toward the blue strips.

6. Measure the length of the quilt and cut two borders from the remaining blue strips to this

7. Make a quilt back approximately 26" x 34". Layer the quilt top with batting and backing. Baste, and then quilt as desired. Trim the excess batting and backing; then bind with the red 2¼"-wide strips.

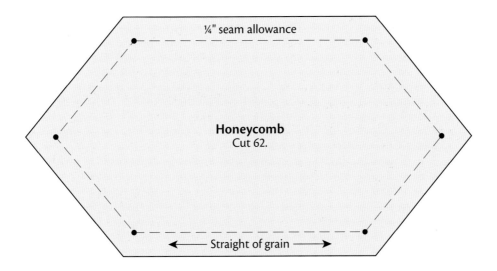

¼" seam allowance

Honeycomb
Cut 62.

← Straight of grain →

We shouldn't get greedy, even if it *is* our favorite flavor of pie. So let yourself admire this pretty table runner and wait until others are offered the last piece before you nab it for your own. And if someone else grabs that last piece, you can console yourself with the knowledge that this table runner went together so quickly you'll have time to make another pie.

Table-runner size: 8¼" x 57¾" ❀ Finished block: 4⅛" x 8¼"

MATERIALS

All yardages are based on 42"-wide fabric. Charm squares are 5" x 5".

8 assorted dark-red print charm squares for blocks

6 assorted dark-green print charm squares for blocks

14 assorted tan or cream charm squares for blocks

⅓ yard of dark-red fabric for binding

⅞ yard of fabric for backing

12" x 60" piece of batting

CUTTING

All measurements include ¼"-wide seam allowances.

From the dark red fabric, cut:
4 strips, 2¼" x 42"

making do

If you don't have a set of precut charm squares, you'll need ¼ yard of a dark-red print, ¼ yard of a dark-green print, and ⅓ yard of a tan or cream print. Cut your own charm squares from these fabrics.

CREATING THE QUILT

1. Place each red charm square right sides together with a tan or cream print charm square. Draw a diagonal line from corner to corner on the wrong side of the light fabrics. Repeat with the green charm squares and the remaining tan or cream squares.

2. Stitch ¼" on each side of the line. Cut in half along the line, creating two matching half-square-triangle units. Press the seam allowances toward the darker fabric. Make eight pairs of red-and-cream half-square-triangle units and six pairs of green-and-cream half-square-triangle units (28 total).

Make 16 red.   Make 12 green.

3. Sew two matching half-square-triangle units together as shown to make a Flying Geese block. Press the seam allowances open. Make eight red blocks and six green blocks.

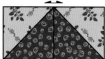 

Make 8 red.   Make 6 green.

4. Sew the Flying Geese blocks together, alternating red and green blocks and rotating them so the points face the center. Press.

5. Make a table-runner back approximately 12" x 60". Layer the table-runner top with batting and backing. Baste, and then quilt as desired. Trim the excess batting and backing and bind the quilt with the red 2¼"-wide strips.

country get-togethers

You can make a long table runner perfect for potlucks or picnics by making 18 Flying Geese blocks. Simply use 18 light-value and 18 dark-value charm squares (we chose to make ours with red and cream fabrics).

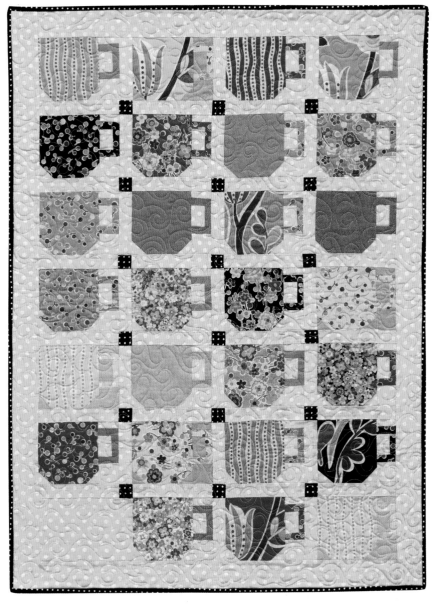

Quilt size: 31" x 41½" ❀ Finished block: 4½" x 6"

This rule may sound outdated, but with the advent of Internet cafes and designer coffees it's more timely than ever. But whether your favorite brew comes from an espresso machine or from a can, you'll enjoy sipping it tucked under this colorful lap quilt.

❀ 33 ❀

MATERIALS

All yardages are based on 42"-wide fabric. Charm squares are 5" x 5". Instructions are simplified to cut all block backgrounds from the yellow-dotted fabric, but you can cut some from additional contrasting charm squares.

27 assorted charm squares for coffee cups (28 if you don't want a blank square)

10 charm squares for handles (use duplicates and fabrics similar to coffee-cup squares)

1¼ yards of yellow-dotted fabric for sashing, blank square, background, and outer border

⅜ yard of black-dotted fabric for cornerstones and binding

1½ yards of fabric for backing

37" x 48" piece of batting

CUTTING

All measurements include ¼"-wide seam allowances.

From *each* of the charm squares for handles, cut:
9 rectangles, 1" x 2" (you'll need 81 for 27 blocks, 84 for 28 blocks)

From the yellow-dotted fabric, cut:
11 strips, 1½" x 42"; crosscut into:

> 54 squares, 1½" x 1½" (56 for 28 blocks)
>
> 27 rectangles, 1½" x 2" (28 for 28 blocks)
>
> 20 rectangles, 1½" x 5" (21 for 28 blocks)
>
> 24 rectangles, 1½" x 6½"

3 strips, 2" x 42"; crosscut into:

> 27 rectangles, 1" x 2" (28 for 28 blocks)
>
> 27 squares, 2" x 2" (28 for 28 blocks)

4 strips, 2½" x 42"; crosscut into:

> 2 strips, 2½" x 38"
>
> 2 strips, 2½" x 31½"

1 rectangle, 5" x 7½" (may substitute 1 pieced block and 1 rectangle, 1½" x 5")

From the black-dotted fabric, cut:
1 strip, 1½" x 42"; crosscut into 18 squares, 1½" x 1½"

4 strips, 2¼" x 42"

CREATING THE QUILT

Each block requires one charm square; three matching or coordinating rectangles, 1" x 2", from charm fabric; and two squares, 1½" x 1½", one square, 2" x 2", one rectangle, 1" x 2", and one rectangle, 1½" x 2", from the background fabric.

We like the unpieced block. If you prefer more symmetry, make 28 blocks instead of 27.

1. Sew yellow-dotted 1½" squares to two adjacent corners of the charm square, right sides together and stitching diagonally from corner to corner. Trim excess fabric from the connector square and press the seam allowances toward the triangles. (See "Connector Squares" on page 74.) Repeat with all the charm squares to make 27 cup units.

2. Match the charm squares with coordinating or matching handle rectangles. Sew a handle 1" x 2" rectangle to a yellow-dotted 1" x 2" rectangle. Sew a matching 1" x 2" rectangle to a yellow-dotted 1½" x 2" rectangle; sew a third matching 1" x 2" rectangle to a yellow-dotted 2" square.

Press each unit toward the darker fabric. Sew the three units together as shown. Press. Make 27 handle units.

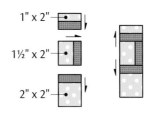

3. Sew a cup unit from step 1 to a coordinating or matching handle unit from step 2 to make a Coffee Cup block. Press toward the coffee-cup unit. Make 27 blocks if you want your quilt to look like ours, or make 28 blocks if you don't want an unpieced square.

Make 27 or 28.

4. Sew four Coffee Cup blocks in a row, inserting a yellow-dotted 1½" x 5" rectangle between each block. Press the seam allowances toward the yellow-dotted fabric. Make six rows with four cups in each row. For the seventh row, sew a yellow-dotted 5" x 7½" rectangle to the left side of the row instead of a block and a yellow rectangle.

5. Alternate and sew together four yellow-dotted 1½" x 6" rectangles and three black-dotted squares. Press the seam allowances toward the yellow-dotted fabric. Make six sashing rows.

6. Sew the block and sashing rows together and press the seam allowances toward the sashing rows.

7. Sew the yellow-dotted 2½" x 38" strips to the sides of the quilt and press the seam allowances toward the strips. Sew the 2½" x 31½" strips to the top and bottom of the quilt and press toward the strips.

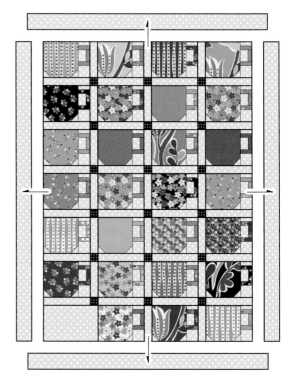

8. Make a quilt back approximately 37" x 48". Layer the quilt top with batting and backing. Baste, and then quilt as desired. Trim the excess batting and backing and bind the quilt with the black-dotted 2¼"-wide strips.

Use a Napkin Only for Your Mouth

Of course there are exceptions. You may also use a napkin to keep something from spilling on your quilt, especially one like this where you can use all of your favorite fabrics.

Quilt size: 30" x 30" ❀ Finished block: 9" x 9"

MATERIAL

All yardages are based on 42"-wide fabric. Charm squares are 5" x 5".

36 assorted charm squares in your favorite prints

⅜ yard of dark fabric for block connector squares and border

⅓ yard of fabric for binding

1⅛ yards of fabric for backing

36" x 36" piece of batting

CUTTING

All measurements include ¼"-wide seam allowances.

From the dark fabric, cut:

2 strips, 2½" x 42"; crosscut into 36 squares, 2½" x 2½"

3 strips, 2" x 42"

From the fabric for binding, cut:

4 strips, 2¼" x 42"

making do

If you don't have a set of precut charm squares, you'll need ¼ yard (or 1 strip, 5" x 42") *each* of a *minimum* of six assorted prints. Cut six charm squares from each print. Additional fabrics will make your quilt look more like our sample.

CREATING THE QUILT

1. Sew a dark 2½" square to one corner of each of the charm squares. Trim the outside corner of the connector square and press the seam allowances toward the triangles. (See "Connector Squares" on page 74.)

Make 36.

2. Sew four of the units from step 1 together to make a block, arranging the dark triangles to meet in the center. Press the seam allowances in opposite directions. Repeat to make nine blocks.

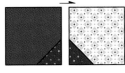 

Make 9.

3. Sew the blocks together into three rows of three blocks per row. Press in opposite directions from row to row. Sew the rows together and press.

4. Measure the length of the quilt, cut two of the dark 2" x 42" strips to this width, and sew them to the sides of the quilt. Press the seam allowances toward the strips. Measure the width of the quilt. Cut the remaining 2"-wide strips to this length and sew them to the top and bottom of the quilt. Press the seam allowances toward the strips.

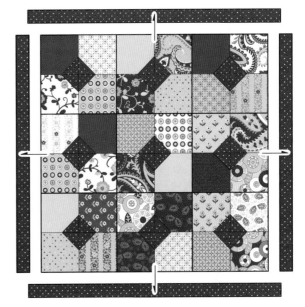

5. Make a quilt back approximately 36" x 36". Layer the quilt top with batting and backing. Baste, and then quilt as desired. Trim the excess batting and backing and bind the quilt with the 2¼" x 42" strips.

These directions make two adorable little table runners. They go together quickly, and one makes a terrific thank-you present to send along with a card. Red and green fabrics give ours a holiday theme, but this pattern looks wonderful with any medium to dark fabrics. Or make it spring-like with pastels against a white background, or summery with colors of the beach. Rich warm colors herald autumn, and bright pink and purple can brighten any winter day.

Quilt size: 2 table runners, 12" x 24", or 1 table mat, 24" x 24"

MATERIALS

Materials will make two table runners or one table mat. All yardages are based on 42"-wide fabric. Charm squares are 5" x 5".

20 assorted charm squares in medium and dark values. Approximately half should be in one color (red) and half in a different color (green).

⅝ yard of red print for border and optional table-runner binding

⅓ yard of beige print for background

⅛ yard of green-striped fabric for cornerstones

1 yard of fabric for backing

30" x 32" piece of batting

CUTTING

Cutting is for two table runners. All measurements include ¼"-wide seam allowances.

From *each* of 16 of the charm squares, cut:
2 rectangles, 2½" x 4½" (32 total)

From *each* of the remaining 4 charm squares, cut:
2 squares, 2½" x 2½" (8 total)

From the beige print, cut:
3 strips, 2½" x 42"; crosscut into:
    32 squares, 2½" x 2½"
    8 rectangles, 2½" x 4½"

From the red print, cut:
4 strips, 2½" x 42"; crosscut into:
    1 strip, 2½" x 20½" (4 total)
    1 strip, 2½" x 8½" (4 total)
4 strips, 2¼" x 42" (optional binding)

From the green-striped fabric, cut:
8 squares, 2½" x 2½"

making do

If you don't have a set of precut charm squares, you'll need a minimum of one fat eighth *each* of four assorted medium or dark prints in two different colors (two green prints and two red prints). Your project will look more like ours if you use at least eight different fabrics total. Cut in strips, 2½" wide, and crosscut into 32 rectangles, 2½" x 4½". Cut eight squares, 2½" x 2½", from the leftover fabric.

CREATING THE QUILT

There are so many options for this project. Instructions are given to make two small table runners. Keep one and give one, or join the table runners along the long edge to make a square table mat. You can also make a long table runner by joining the pieced units together lengthwise, or place mats by deleting the side borders and cornerstones.

1. Sew a beige 2½" square to one corner of each 2½" x 4½" rectangle as shown. Trim the outside corner of the connector square and press the seam allowances toward the triangles. (See "Connector Squares" on page 74.) Sew all the squares to red units with the seams slanting one direction and all the squares sewn to green units with the seams slanting in the opposite direction. Press the seam allowances on the red rectangles toward the red fabric and on the green rectangles toward the beige fabric.

Make 16.   Make 16.

2. In the same manner, sew a red or green 2½" square to one corner of each beige rectangle. Sew four in one direction and four in the opposite direction.

Make 4.   Make 4.

3. Sew a red unit from step 1 to a green unit from step 1. Press the seam allowances open. Repeat with all the units from step 1.

Make 16.

4. Sew four of the units from step 3 together. Repeat to make four rows. Sew a unit from step 2 to each end of each row, being careful to choose a unit that slants in the correct direction. Sew two of the resulting rows together to make the center of one table runner. Repeat to make two centers. Press the seam allowances open.

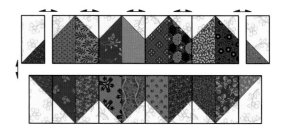

5. Sew the red 2½" x 20½" strips to the top and bottom of the two table runners. Press the seam allowances toward the red fabric. If you want 12" x 20" place mats, just layer, quilt, and bind. Otherwise, sew a green 2½" square to each end of the red 2½" x 8½" strips. Sew these to each side of the table runners. Press the seam allowances toward the red fabric.

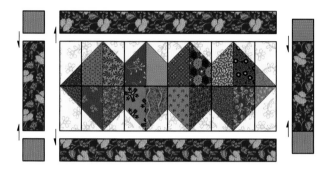

6. Make two backs and cut two pieces of batting approximately 18" x 24". Layer the table runners with batting and backing. Baste, and then quilt as desired. Trim the excess batting and backing and bind the table runners with the red 2¼"-wide strips.

country choices

This project has several different variations, and if you buy a couple of charm packs, you can make matching table linens. For a center table mat, sew the two table runners together along the long sides. Make the back 30" x 30", and use that same size for your batting.

Or make one long table runner (12" x 44") by sewing the two center pieces together. Sew one side border to each center piece and cut the top and bottom borders to 2½" x 40½".

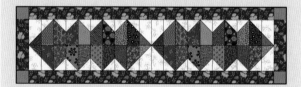

Regardless of the project you make, you can either finish the table runners with binding, or leave the binding off, cut the backing and batting about ½" larger than your top, and finish each runner as follows.

1. Layer the batting, followed by the backing, right side up, and then the top, right side down. Stitch around the table runner using a ¼" seam allowance, leaving part of one end open for turning.

2. Trim the backing and batting to the quilt-top edge and clip the corners. Turn right side out and stitch the opening closed using a hand whipstitch. Quilt ¼" around the outside edge to stabilize and quilt the rest of the table runner as desired.

People Will Find You Interesting If You're Interested in Them

Quilt size: 15" x 19" ❀ Finished block: 3" x 3"

If you're shy talking to people you don't know, ask them questions about themselves. Or show off this quilt—it can spark a conversation. It may be a little fussier than most of the quilts in this book, but the small size makes it a perfect project to practice your points.

MATERIALS

All yardages are based on 42"-wide fabric. Charm squares are 5" x 5".

30 assorted medium- to dark-value charm squares for blocks and pieced border

18 assorted light- to medium-value charm squares for block backgrounds

¼ yard of pink print for side and corner triangles

¼ yard of brown print for binding

⅝ yard of fabric for backing

20" x 24" piece of batting

CUTTING

All measurements include ¼"-wide seam allowances.

From *each* of 18 medium- to dark-value charm squares, cut:
1 square, 2⅞" x 2⅞"; cut each square in half diagonally to make 2 triangles (36 total)

3 squares, 1⅞" x 1⅞"; cut each square in half diagonally to make 2 triangles (108 total)

From the remaining 12 medium- to dark-value charm squares, cut:
4 squares, 1⅞" x 1⅞"; cut each square in half diagonally to make 2 triangles (96 total, 4 will be extra)

From *each* of the light- to medium-value charm squares, cut:
2 squares, 1⅞" x 1⅞"; cut each square in half diagonally to make 2 triangles (72 total)

1 square, 1½" x 1½" (18 total)

From the pink print, cut:
3 squares, 6" x 6"; cut each square into quarters diagonally to make 12 triangles (2 are extra)

2 squares, 4½" x 4½"; cut each square in half diagonally to make 2 triangles (4 total)

From the brown print, cut:
2 strips, 2¼" x 42"

making do

If you don't have a set of precut charm squares, you'll need one fat eighth (9" x 20") *each* of nine assorted medium- to dark-value fabrics. Cut two 2⅞" squares and eleven 1⅞" squares from each fabric; you may need a couple of additional small squares for the border. You'll also need one fat eighth *each* of six assorted light- to medium-value fabrics for the backgrounds. Cut six 1⅞" squares and three 1½" squares from each fabric.

CREATING THE QUILT

Each block is made from two medium/dark 2⅞" triangles, four medium/dark 1⅞" triangles, four light/medium 1⅞" triangles, and one light/medium 1½" square. Many, but not all of the blocks have matching light/medium pieces.

1. Sew two different 2⅞" triangles together, being careful not to stretch the bias edges. Press the seam allowances in one direction. Repeat with all the 2⅞" triangles to make 18 half-square-triangle units.

Make 18.

2. Pair four matching light/medium 1⅞" triangles and four assorted medium/dark triangles. Sew the triangle pairs together and press the seam allowances in one direction. Make 72 half-square-triangle units for the blocks. Repeat with the remaining 1⅞" triangles to make approximately 64 additional units for the borders.

Make 72   Make 64
for blocks. for borders.

3. Sew a unit from step 1, four half-square-triangle units from step 2, and a light/medium 1½" square together to make a block. Press as indicated. Make 18 blocks. Many (but not all) of our blocks have the same light/medium background fabric, and we find this helps the individual blocks show more clearly.

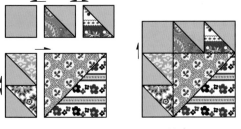

Make 18.

4. Arrange the blocks, side triangles, and corner triangles as shown. Sew the blocks and side triangles into diagonal rows. The pink triangles are cut oversized and will extend beyond the pieced blocks. Sew the rows together and add the pink 4½" triangles on each corner. Trim the quilt top ¼" outside the block corners.

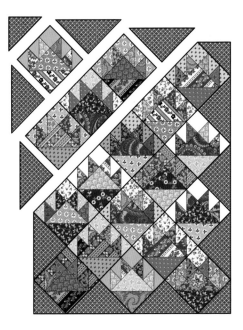

5. Sew 13 half-square-triangle units together, orienting the triangles in the same direction. Make two units and sew one to the top and one to the bottom of the quilt. Sew 19 half-square-triangle units together for each side border. We don't worry about fitting everything together perfectly. With this many seams, it can be difficult to make the borders exactly the same size as the quilt center. Do as we do: if it's too long, cut if off. If it's too short, add more triangle units! You can also adjust the lengths by taking a little larger or smaller seam allowance between some of the triangle squares. Can you see which of these methods we used?

6. Make a quilt back approximately 20" x 24". Layer the quilt top with batting and backing. Baste, and then quilt as desired. Trim the excess batting and backing and bind the quilt with the brown 2¼"-wide strips.

Quilt size: 40" x 45" ❀ Finished block: 4" x 4½" ❀ Tree-skirt diameter: 40"

You can make either a tree skirt or a pretty quilt—or buy two charm packs and make both! Maybe after all the ladies open their gifts you'll be able to see the tree skirt that's been buried under packages all those weeks.

MATERIALS

All yardages are based on 42"-wide fabric. Charm squares are 5" x 5".

50 Christmas-print charm squares, 5" x 5"

1⅛ yards of white fabric

⅔ yard of red print for binding tree skirt **OR** ⅜ yard of red print for binding quilt

2½ yards of fabric for backing

44" x 49" piece of batting

1 yard of string and chalk wheel or chalk pencil

CUTTING

Measurements include ¼"-wide seam allowances.

From each of the 50 charm squares, cut:
2 rectangles, 2½" x 5" (100 total, 1 will be extra)

From the white fabric, cut:
7 strips, 5" x 42"; crosscut each strip into 16 rectangles, 2½" x 5" (112 total, 13 will be extra)

From the red print, cut:
2¼"-wide bias strips, enough to yield 180" of binding for tree skirt

OR 5 strips, 2¼" x 42", for quilt binding

making do

If you don't have a set of precut charm squares, you'll need one 2½" x 42" strip *each* of 16 different red, green, and tan prints. Cut seven rectangles, 2½" x 5", from each print (112 total; 12 will be extra).

CREATING THE QUILT

1. Sew the charm rectangles and white rectangles together in pairs to make pieced units as shown. Press the seam allowances toward the charm rectangles.

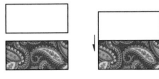

Make 99.

2. Arrange the units from step 1 in 11 rows of 9 units each. Sew the units together in rows. Press the seam allowances in opposite direction from row to row, and then sew the rows together; press.

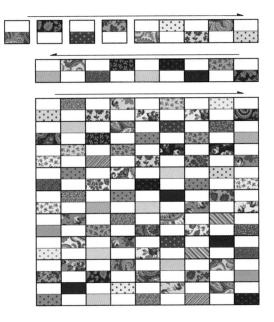

3. Layer the quilt top with batting and backing; baste. Quilt closely.

4. If you don't want to make a tree skirt, simply bind the quilt with the red 2¼"-wide strips and enjoy it. Otherwise, proceed to step 5.

5. Fasten one end of the string around your chalk wheel or chalk pencil.

6. Lay the quilt on a flat surface. Find the middle of the quilt and mark it with a pin. Hold the chalk marker at the midpoint of a long edge of the quilt and pull the string taut to the center of the quilt. Hold the string firmly in place at the center of the

quilt and swing the chalk marker around the quilt top to mark a circle that's approximately 40" in diameter.

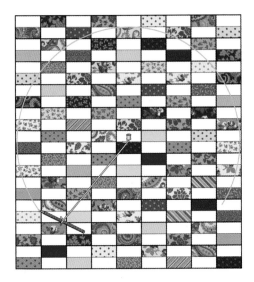

7. Cut the circle on the marked line.

8. Trim the string to about 4" long and repeat to mark an 8"-diameter circle in the center of the quilt.

9. Cut a slit from the outer edge of the quilt circle to the center point. Then cut out the center circle.

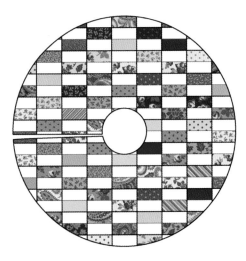

10. Using the red 2¼"-wide bias strips, bind the raw edges. Start at the inner edge of the slit, work around the outer perimeter, and stitch back up the other side of the slit. (See "Bias Binding" on page 77.) Starting with a new length of binding, leave a tail for a tie; then bind the center circle and leave a tail at the other end of the opening for the tie. Press under the raw edges on the ties and topstitch close to the open edge.

Gloves seem too formal to wear while seated at a table covered with this little quilt. It's a casual, scrappy quilt that would make anyone feel at ease.

Quilt size: 24" x 31" ❖ Finished block: 4" x 4"

MATERIALS

All yardages are based on 42"-wide fabric. Charm squares are 5" x 5".

42 assorted charm squares in cream, tan, pink, brown, and red for blocks and border

½ yard of dark print for block squares and binding

1 yard of fabric for backing

30" x 37" piece of batting

CUTTING

All measurements include ¼"-wide seam allowances.

From each charm square, cut:*

1 rectangle, 3" x 4½"

1 rectangle, 2" x 3"

1 square, 2" x 2" (You only need 32)

From the dark print, cut:

2 strips, 2" x 42"; crosscut into 42 squares, 2" x 2"**

3 strips, 2¼" x 42"

Keep pieces of the same fabric together.

**If you have less than 42" of usable fabric you'll need to cut 3 strips.*

making do

If you don't have a set of precut charm squares, you'll need one fat eighth (9" x 20") *each* of seven assorted prints. Cut six 2" x 3" rectangles, six 3" x 4½" rectangles, and six 2" squares from each fabric.

CREATING THE QUILT

Each block uses a dark print 2" square plus a 3" x 4½" rectangle and a 2" x 3" rectangle of the same fabric.

1. Sew a dark print 2" square to a charm fabric 2" x 3" rectangle. Press seam allowances toward the dark print. Sew a matching 3" x 4½" rectangle to this unit to make a block. Press toward the larger rectangle. Make 42 blocks.

Make 42.

2. Sew the blocks together in seven rows of six blocks in each row, orienting the blocks as shown. Press the seam allowances in opposite directions from row to row. Sew the rows together and press.

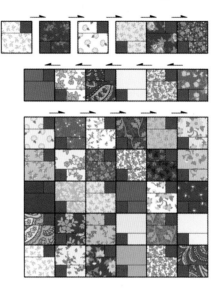

country angles

We arranged the blocks in diagonal rows according to color or light, medium, and dark value.

3. Sew 16 charm fabric 2" squares together to make a border for the top of the quilt. Repeat for the bottom border, adjusting seams as necessary to fit the quilt. Sew the borders to the top and bottom of the quilt and press the seam allowances away from the borders.

4. Make a quilt back approximately 30" x 37". Layer the quilt top with batting and backing. Baste, and then quilt as desired. Trim the excess batting and backing and bind the quilt with the dark print 2¼"-wide strips.

Quilt size: 32½" x 52" ❀ Finished block: 6½" x 6½"

Lateness may be rudeness unless it pertains to getting a quilt done in time for a gift. In that case, the normal definition of late is very flexible. For example, giving a child's quilt on the baby's first birthday when you intended to have it for the newborn is perfectly acceptable. Giving it at high school graduation might be considered a bit late.

MATERIALS

All yardages are based on 42"-wide fabric. Charm squares are 5" x 5".

40 assorted charm squares

⅝ yard of gold print for block frames

⅝ yard of orange print for block frames

¼ yard of dark-red print for block corners

¼ yard of light diagonally striped fabric for block corners

½ yard of red print for binding

1¾ yards of fabric for backing

38" x 60" piece of batting

CUTTING

All measurements include ¼"-wide seam allowances.

From the gold print, cut:
2 strips, 5" x 42"
5 strips, 1½" x 42"; crosscut into 40 rectangles, 1½" x 5"

From the orange print, cut:
2 strips, 5" x 42"
5 strips, 1½" x 42"; crosscut into 40 rectangles, 1½" x 5"

From the dark-red print, cut:
4 strips, 1½" x 42"

From the diagonally striped fabric, cut:
4 strips, 1½" x 42"

From the red print, cut:
5 strips, 2¼" x 42"

making do

This is one of the quilts in this book that looks best with a lot of different fabrics, so we recommend you use at least 10 different prints. Ten Layer Cakes (10" x 10" squares) can each be cut into four block centers, or troll through your stash to see if you can find ten fabrics from which to cut a 5" x 20" strip, and then cut four charm squares from each strip.

CREATING THE QUILT

1. Sew a dark red 1½" x 42" strip to each long side of a gold 5" x 42" strip. Make two strip sets and press the seam allowances toward the gold strips. Crosscut the strip sets into 80 units, 1½" wide. Repeat with the orange 5" x 42" strips and diagonally striped 1½" x 42" strips. Press the seam allowances toward the diagonally striped fabric.

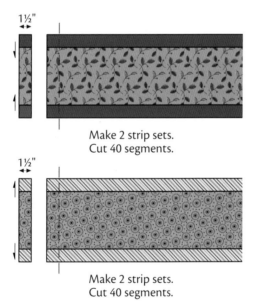

1½"

Make 2 strip sets.
Cut 40 segments.

1½"

Make 2 strip sets.
Cut 40 segments.

2. Sew a gold 1½" x 5" rectangle to each side of a charm square. Press the seam allowances toward the gold rectangles. Sew dark red and gold units from step 1 to the top and the bottom of the charm square. Press toward the center of the block. Make 20 blocks with dark red and gold fabric frames. Repeat to make 20 blocks with orange

and diagonally striped fabric frames, pressing the seam allowances in the opposite directions.

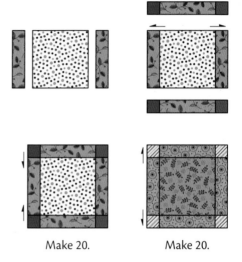

Make 20.   Make 20.

3. Arrange the blocks into eight rows of five blocks in each row, alternating the blocks with gold frames and the blocks with orange frames. Sew the blocks together, pressing the seam allowances in opposite directions from row to row. Sew the rows together and press.

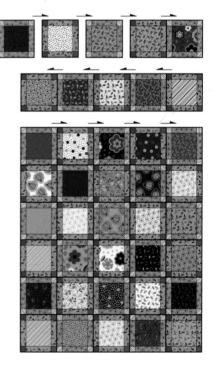

4. Make a quilt back approximately 38" x 60". Layer the quilt top with batting and backing. Baste, and then quilt as desired. Trim the excess batting and backing and bind the quilt with the red print 2¼"-wide strips.

Quilt size: 34" x 40" ✿ Finished block: 3" x 3"

MATERIALS

All yardages are based on 42"-wide fabric. Charm squares are 5" x 5".

80 assorted charm squares for blocks

½ yard of pink print for inner border

½ yard of turquoise print for outer border

⅓ yard of green fabric for binding

1⅓ yards of fabric for backing

40" x 46" piece of batting

Template plastic **OR** Lil' Twister acrylic template (available from your local quilt shop or Country Threads)

If you were a fidgety or restless child, chances are you've heard this rule! On the other hand, tilted blocks are not only attractive in quilts, they're much easier to make than they look.

CUTTING

All measurements include ¼"-wide seam allowances.

From the pink print, cut:
5 strips, 3¼" x 42"

From the turquoise print, cut:
4 strips, 4" x 42"

From the green fabric, cut:
4 strips, 2¼" x 42"

making do

If you don't have a set of precut charm squares, you'll need a minimum of one strip, 5" x 42", each from 10 different prints. Cut eight squares, 5" x 5" from each fabric.

CREATING THE QUILT

1. Sew the charm squares together in 10 rows of eight charm squares in each row. Press the seam allowances in opposite directions from row to row. Try and place charm squares with good contrast next to each other.

2. Sew the pink 3¼"-wide strips together to make a long strip. Cut two borders the length of the quilt and sew them to the sides of the quilt center. Cut two borders the width of the quilt and sew them to the top and bottom of the center. Press the seam allowances toward the borders.

3. If you don't have the acrylic template, cut a square of template plastic, 3½" x 3½". Make a mark on each side of the square 1" from the corner. Connect the marks diagonally to make a tilted "X" on the template square.

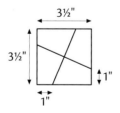

4. Place the template on the quilt top made in steps 1 and 2. Align the marks on the template with the seam lines; the template square will be tilted at an angle to the seams. Cut along each side of the template to make a tilted block. Repeat with all the seam intersections, including the pink borders. It's helpful to place the blocks on a work wall as you cut them to keep them in order. You'll have a total of 99 tilted blocks.

5. Keeping them in order, sew the blocks together in 11 rows of nine blocks in each row. Press the seam allowances in opposite directions from row to row. Cut two turquoise 4"-wide strips the width of the quilt top and sew them to the top and bottom of the quilt. Cut the remaining turquoise strips the length of the quilt and sew them to the sides. Press toward the borders.

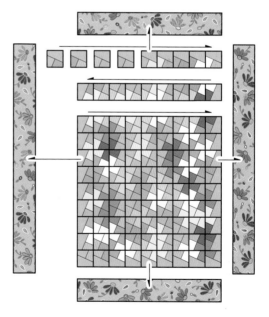

6. Make a quilt back approximately 40" x 46". Layer the quilt top with batting and backing. Baste, and then quilt as desired. Trim the excess batting and backing and bind the quilt with the green 2¼"-wide strips.

Quilt size: 16½" x 51½" ❀ Finished block: 2½" x 2¾"

Leaving your napkin on the chair is one of those silent signals, like placing your utensil horizontally across your plate to signal you're finished with a course during a meal, or giving this pretty little quilt to say, "Congratulations," or, "I love you."

MATERIALS

All yardages are based on 42"-wide fabric. Charm squares are 5" x 5".

36 assorted charm squares for blocks and pieced backing

1 yard of red fabric for background and binding

¼ yard of cream print for sashing strips

¾ yard of fabric for backing

22" x 56" piece of batting

Template plastic **OR** acrylic house-shaped template (available from Country Threads)

CUTTING

All measurements include ¼"-wide seam allowances. House pattern is on page 63. Refer to "Working with Templates" on page 74 if needed.

From each charm square, cut:*
2 house pieces (72 total)

1 square, 1½" x 1½"

1 triangle, 3¼" on short sides. See diagram below.

From the red fabric, cut:
7 strips, 3" x 42"; from these strips cut 84 house pieces (Cut strips 3¼" x 42" if using the acrylic template.)

4 strips, 2¼" x 42"

From the cream print, cut:
5 strips, 1½" x 17"

*Accuracy when cutting shapes is required since there's little extra fabric in a charm square. Cut the house pieces first. The other two pieces are for the back of the quilt and are optional.

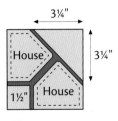

Charm square

making do

If you don't have a set of precut charm squares, you'll need a minimum of one 3½" x 20" strip from each of 12 assorted fabrics. Cut each strip into six house shapes.

CREATING THE QUILT

1. Mark the dots from the house pattern on the wrong side of all of the house pieces. Place a charm-fabric house piece right sides together with a red house piece. Notice that in order to sew the seam, one of the house pieces is rotated 90°. Join the two pieces along one side of the "roof." Start and stop at the dots, backstitching for a stitch or two at each end. Be careful to not sew into the seam allowances. Press toward the background. Repeat for all 72 charm-fabric house pieces. You'll have 12 red house pieces remaining.

Make 72.

2. Arrange six units from step 1 in a row. Flip one unit so it lies right sides together with an adjacent unit and sew the first two edges together. Stop at the dot with the needle in the down position and rotate the two units so you can sew along the next edges.

Stop at the next dot, rotate the units, and sew the final adjacent edges together. Press the seam allowances open. Make 12 rows with six charm-fabric houses in each row. Sew an additional red house piece at the end of each row.

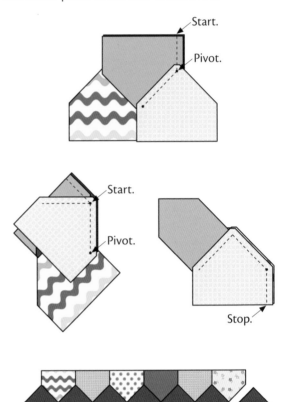

3. Trim the red house pieces at the ends of the rows even with the charm-fabric house pieces.

Make 12.

4. Lay out the house rows and the five cream 1½" x 17" strips as shown. Sew the rows and sashing strips together, pressing toward the cream strips.

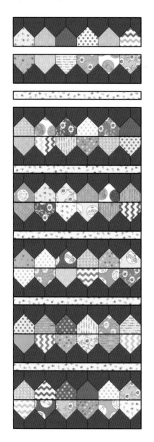

5. Make a quilt back approximately 22" x 56". Layer the quilt top with batting and backing. Baste, and then quilt as desired. Trim the excess batting and backing and bind the quilt with the red 2¼"-wide red strips.

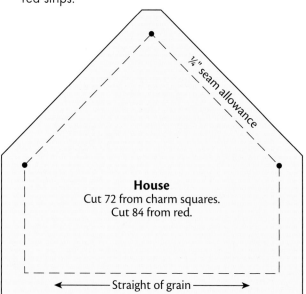

House
Cut 72 from charm squares.
Cut 84 from red.

¼" seam allowance

← Straight of grain →

country thrift

If you like to utilize as much of the fabric in each charm square as possible, you can always use the leftovers for the back of the quilt. Piece the 3¼" triangles together along the long diagonal, sew the triangles together, and make mini borders with the 1½" squares. Sew this unit in the center of the quilt back, and you not only have the satisfaction of using every bit of your charm fabric, but you also have a very pretty quilt back!

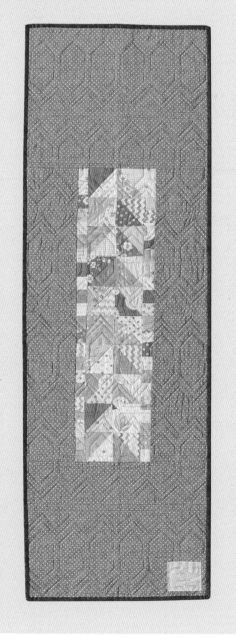

Don't Play with Table Utensils

Quilt size: 13¼" x 26¼" ❀ Finished block: 4⅜" x 4⅜"

But didn't your little brother or cousin look cute with a spoon balanced on the end of his nose? Almost as cute as this little wall quilt or table runner!

The instructions here are for a table runner. But if you buy 35 light and 35 dark charm squares, you'll have enough to make a five square by seven square table topper. For three place mats, three squares by four squares each, buy 36 light and 36 dark charm squares.

MATERIALS

All yardages are based on 42"-wide fabric. Charm squares are 5" x 5".

17 assorted light-value charm squares

17 dark-value red and blue charm squares (our pack had 16 red, 16 blue, and 1 tan)

¼ yard of blue print for binding

½ yard of fabric for backing

18" x 30" piece of batting

CUTTING

All measurements include ¼"-wide seam allowances.

From each charm square, cut:
4 strips, 1⅛" x 5" (136 total)*

From the blue print, cut:
3 strips, 2¼" x 42"

Keep strips of the same fabric together.

making do

If you don't have a set of precut charm squares, you'll need one 5" x 15" strip each of a minimum of six different dark-value prints and a 5 x 20" strip each of five different light-value prints. Cut your charm squares from these fabrics.

CREATING THE QUILT

Each block is made from one light and one dark fabric.

1. Sew four dark 1⅛" x 5" strips alternated with three light 1⅛" x 5" strips. You'll have one light strip left over. Press the seam allowances toward the dark strips. Make 17 blocks.

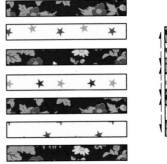 

Make 17.

2. Measure the average height of the blocks. They should be about 4⅞". Trim the width of the blocks to match the height so the blocks are square (4⅞" x 4⅞").

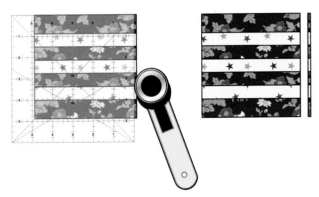

3. Sew seven of the remaining light-value strips together to make one block and trim it to the size of the other blocks.

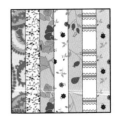

4. Arrange the blocks in six rows of three blocks in each row, rotating the blocks to run horizontally and vertically. Sew together in rows, pressing the seam allowances in opposite directions from row to row. Sew the rows together and press.

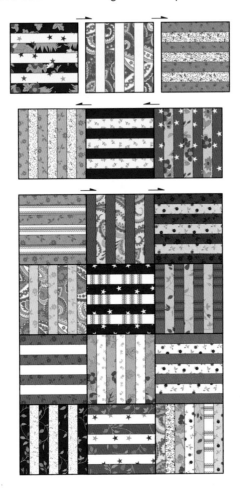

5. Make a quilt back approximately 18" x 30". Layer the quilt top with batting and backing. Baste, and then quilt as desired. Trim the excess batting and backing and bind the quilt with the blue 2¼"-wide strips.

Our kitties are meticulous when it comes to their whiskers, and we hope you gentlemen are too. In our pillow, the raw edges fray to form little whiskers around each circle. We'd never get cream on them!

Pillow size: 19" x 19"

MATERIALS

All yardages are based on 42"-wide fabric. Charm squares are 5" x 5".

42 assorted charm squares

⅔ yard of pink fabric for pillow front and back

20" x 20" piece of batting

20" x 20" pillow form*

*You can purchase an inexpensive bed pillow for the stuffing. Using this squishable pillow in a smaller-size case will create a very plump pillow.

CUTTING

From the pink fabric, cut:
2 squares, 20" x 20"

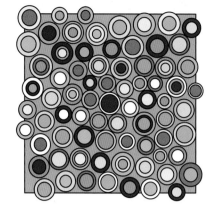

making do

If you don't have a set of precut charm squares, use your leftover scraps to cut about 160 circles freehand. The circles can be almost any size up to about 3" in diameter. Perfection is not required!

CREATING THE PILLOW

1. From each charm square, cut four circles freehand. You don't need to be precise. Circles can measure from 1½" to about 3" in diameter.

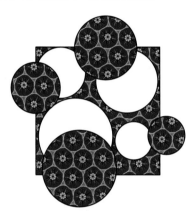

2. Position a large circle in the center of a pink 20" square, right sides facing up. Machine stitch ⅛" to ¼" inside the circle's edge, leaving a raw edge. Lay a smaller circle on top and stitch ⅛" to ¼" inside the smaller circle's edge.

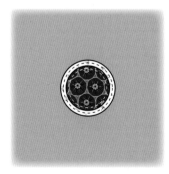

3. Continue sewing circles in a very casual and random pattern all over the pillow top. Position some circles at the edge of the square so they extend over the edge. Go back and randomly add a third circle to the stacks if you have any small circles left over.

4. Layer the remaining pink 20" square right side up over the piece of batting. Machine quilt in an allover stipple or grid pattern to make the pillow back.

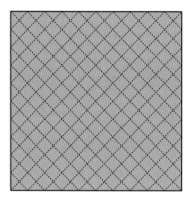

5. Lay the pillow top and back right sides together. Trim away any circles extending beyond the edge of the pillow top. Machine stitch around the edge using a ¼" seam allowance, leaving a 3" to 4" opening unsewn. If you use a bed pillow, leave an opening large enough to stuff the pillow into the pillow top.

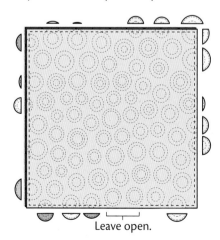
Leave open.

6. Turn right side out, wash in a washing machine, and dry in a dryer so the raw edges of the circles fray and ripple. Stuff the pillow and stitch closed by hand.

Quilt size: 33" x 37½" ❀ Finished block: 4½" x 4½"

Like the Golden Rule, this quilt is so basic we hesitated to even give instructions for it, but sometimes it helps to have all the yardage and trimming written down for you. When we need to make a quilt as quickly as possible—for comfort, for love, or just for warmth—this is the pattern we turn to.

MATERIALS

All yardages are based on 42"-wide fabric. Charm squares are 5" x 5".

42 charm squares for blocks

½ yard of turquoise print for border

⅓ yard of pink print for binding

1¼ yards of fabric for backing

39" x 44" piece of batting

CUTTING

All measurements include ¼"-wide seam allowances.

From the turquoise print, cut:

4 strips, 3½" x 42"

From the pink print, cut:

4 strips, 2¼" x 42"

making do

Make this quilt with 2 fabrics or 42. Use scraps, 11 Layer Cakes (10" x 10" squares), or yardage. For a two-fabric checkerboard, you'll need ½ yard each of two contrasting fabrics, and then cut 21 charm squares from each.

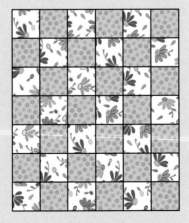

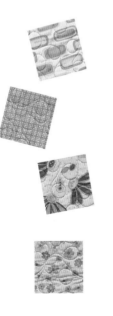

CREATING THE QUILT

1. Sew the charm squares into seven rows of six squares in each row. Press the seam allowances in opposite directions from row to row.

2. Measure the length of the quilt, cut two of the turquoise 3½"-wide strips to that measurement, and sew to the sides of the quilt top. Press the seam allowances toward the turquoise strips. Measure the width of the quilt, cut two of the 3½"-wide strips to that measurement, and sew to the top and bottom of the quilt. Press toward the turquoise strips.

3. Make a quilt back approximately 39" x 44". Layer the quilt top with batting and backing. Baste, and then quilt as desired. Trim the excess batting and backing and bind the quilt with the pink 2¼"-wide strips.

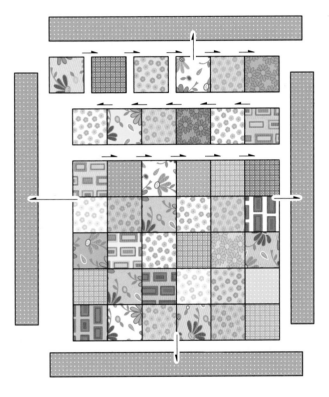

Charm School Techniques

The fabrics in a charm pack blend beautifully, but are limited in number, color, and value.

Most of the quilts in this book use basic quiltmaking skills, but here are a few tips that may help.

WORKING WITH CHARM SQUARES

Charm-square packets are becoming more popular every year. We can't resist the wonderful fabrics in coordinating patterns and colors. The downside is that a pack with specific fabrics may be available for only a short period of time, so the chance of finding charm packs just like the ones we used to make the quilts in this book is slim. In addition, you're working with a limited number of fabrics and won't be able to control how much of each color or value you have. If you're short a few squares, look through your stash and those bags of scraps you can't bear to throw out. Your homemade charm squares don't have to match perfectly. Variety adds a little spice to your mix. You'll also see some quilts where we didn't have enough charms to piece a block, so we simply put in a plain square of background fabric.

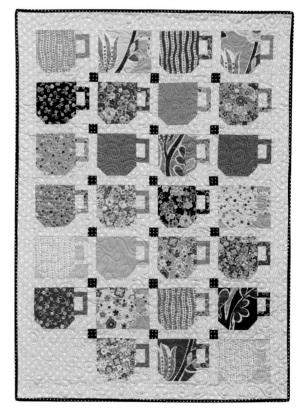

Even though the plain square breaks up the quilt design, it's not the first thing you see. It blends in and looks like part of the design.

When deciding which fabric to use for a specific piece, look at your charm squares in terms of whether the individual squares blend together or are easy to tell apart. Red and yellow are two colors that often "pop" and stand out from other colors. Differences in value, whether the squares are lighter or darker than each other, instead of color differences often create a quilt design. Squint at your charm squares or view them in dim light to distinguish different values.

Your charm pack probably won't be evenly divided into different values or colors. Ours weren't either! Look at the photos of our quilts, and you'll see some blocks where the individual pieces blend together and others where they're distinct. It's all a matter of "making do with what you have," just as quilters have done for many years.

CUTTING

Charm School has really only one rule: Cut charms carefully!

Some of the projects use every bit of each charm square, so there's no room for mis-cuts. We suggest you use a new blade in your rotary cutter and take your time measuring and cutting. If you do ruin a charm square, don't panic! Chances are there's something in your stash you can use as a substitute.

Some charm squares have pinked edges, and the 5" measurement goes to the outside edge of the pinking, as do seam allowances. If you don't need to use all 5", you can trim off the pinked edges—but double-check to be certain before you cut.

CONNECTOR SQUARES

In our quilt designs, we often use connector squares as an easy way of adding triangle corners to rectangles or larger squares. This is especially true if the desired finished triangle is very small. Our thanks to Mary Ellen Hopkins for teaching us about connector squares.

1. Use a pencil or chalk to mark a diagonal line from corner to corner on the wrong side of the connector square. If the square is small, you may not need to mark the line. Place the connector

square against the background piece, right sides together, in the desired corner (unless directed otherwise in the quilt directions).

2. Stitch diagonally across the square, stitching on the line from corner to corner.

3. Trim away the outside corner of the connector square. Do not cut off the corner of the background block. Leaving the background block intact helps keep your piecing precise. Fold the connector square back over the seam and press.

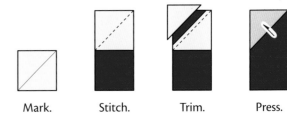

Mark.   Stitch.   Trim.   Press.

WORKING WITH TEMPLATES

Most of the projects in this book are designed for rotary cutting, but some require templates, the patterns for which appear in the projects. Some also have acrylic templates available for purchase at your local quilt shop or Country Threads. They make cutting uniform pieces easy, since you don't have to worry about slicing off pieces of your template material. You can make your own templates from plastic or heavy cardstock. Template plastic is easy to see through, so tracing the shape is quick and simple. If you use cardstock, hold the pattern against a light source, like a window, to see the pattern. Use a permanent marking pen to trace the pattern shape onto the template material. Use paper or craft scissors to cut along the line. Mark the pattern name and grain line on the right side of the template and mark seam intersections to make joining pieces easier. All our patterns for piecing include $\frac{1}{4}$" seam allowances.

If the pattern is not symmetrical, take care that both the fabric and the template are right side up before marking and cutting; otherwise the piece will be the wrong shape. Place the template on the right side of the fabric and with a pencil or removable fabric pen, trace around the edges and mark the seam intersections. Cut along the line. If the lines of the pattern are straight, you can stack up to six fabrics and cut all six at once with a rotary cutter and ruler.

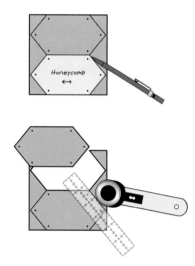

BORDERS

You've probably noticed many of our quilts don't have borders. We like to add borders that enhance the quilt, though sometimes we confess we'll add them to make the quilt larger. Even if that's your motivation, choose borders that complement the quilt and don't overwhelm the piecing.

1. If the borders need to be more than 40" long, sew the strips together to make one long strip. If the quilt blocks have dominant diagonal lines, we might sew the strips together on the diagonal as we do binding (see "Double-Fold Binding" on page 76). Usually, a straight seam looks just fine. Press the seam allowances open.

2. Measure the length of the quilt top through the center and cut two border strips to that measurement. Sew them to the sides of the quilt, matching the centers and ends. Seam allowances are usually pressed toward the borders.

3. Measure the width of the quilt top through the center, including the borders just added. Cut two border strips to that measurement and sew them to the top and the bottom of the quilt, matching the centers and ends. Seam allowances are usually pressed toward the borders.

FINISHING

You might like to send your larger quilts to a professional quilter, but these quilts are small enough that it's easy to finish them yourself.

Layering the Quilt

The quilt sandwich consists of backing, batting, and the quilt top. Cut the batting and backing at least 2" to 4" larger than the quilt top. We sometimes use low-loft, dense fleece instead of batting for wall hangings and table runners.

1. Spread the backing, wrong side up, on a flat, clean surface. Anchor the edges with masking tape. Be careful not to stretch the backing out of shape.

2. Spread the batting over the backing, smoothing out any wrinkles.

3. Place the pressed quilt top on the batting, right side up. Smooth out any wrinkles and make sure the edges of the quilt top are parallel to the edges of the backing.

Mary and Janey; photo by Susan Henderson

Connie and Lucy; photo by Roy Tesene

I've lived on the Country Threads farm for 32 years and love my life in the country! I also love animals and am active in dog transport and rescue. I drive my "leg" of a transport many Saturdays or Sundays, meeting the previous driver who brings the dogs to a meeting place near my home. We transfer the dogs to my van and I drive them north about 70 miles to another parking lot, where someone meets me and takes the dogs to the Minneapolis area. There the dogs live in foster homes belonging to members of the rescue groups who have arranged to have them pulled from kill shelters in the south. The search then begins to find each dog a forever home.

I have four rescued dogs: Izzy, a golden doodle; Maggie, a golden retriever; Janey, a Jack Russell terrier; and Benjie, a schnauzer mix. My next endeavor will be a cage-free dog-boarding business on the Country Threads farm.

I live just three miles from Mary's farm in Garner with my husband, Roy; two cats; and Lucy, our yellow Lab. We raised our three boys in this town of 3000 people, and now our kids and grandkids come for visits and are amazed at the freedoms small-town life can bring.

I've always loved to garden, and several years ago I participated in the Master Gardener program. Our 100-year-old home is surrounded by huge shade trees, so I've planted dozens and dozens of hosta varieties. I still sew every day and love it. My sewing room is located above our three-stall garage and is full of fabric in old cupboards. We are blessed at Country Threads not only with wonderful fabric, but with great friends, customers, employees, animals, and plants. As the saying goes, "Is this Heaven? No, it's Iowa!"

Country Threads is truly located on a farm in northern Iowa!

Connie Tesene and Mary Etherington have been business partners at Country Threads since 1983, shortly after both moved to Garner, Iowa. The business started as a wholesale quilt-pattern company that soon expanded into a retail quilt shop on Mary's small farm in north-central Iowa. Today the farm is home to the quilt shop, the wholesale operation, the machine-quilting business, and numerous farm animals, many of whom will greet you when you arrive. Camp is held several times a year in the haymow of the barn, where friends from across the nation gather to sew together for four days.

Connie and Mary have published over 800 individual patterns and more than 20 quilt-pattern books. Even though the business has expanded over the past 28 years, the farm is still home to fancy chickens, geese, goats, dogs, and cats. Visitors enjoy the interaction with the cats in the quilt shop and come to know the pets on a personal basis through the *Goat Gazette* newsletter and the free email newsletter.

Country Threads' mission statement: where no goat has ever been denied, no cat has ever been disciplined, and where no dog has ever been discouraged . . . and where quilting is alive and well!

There's More Online!

If you agree with Country Threads' mission statement, you're going to love your visit to the farm—or to the website at www.countrythreads.com.

For more great books on quilting and sewing, visit www.martingale-pub.com.